THE BILL OF RIGHTS

SIXTH AMENDMENT: THE RIGHT TO A FAIR TRIAL

BY RICH SMITH

SERIES CONSULTANT: SCOTT HARR, J.D. CRIMINAL JUSTICE
DEPARTMENT CHAIR, CONCORDIA UNIVERSITY ST. PAUL

VISIT US AT
WWW.ABDOPUBLISHING.COM

Published by ABDO Publishing Company, 8000 West 78th Street, Suite 310, Edina, MN 55439.
Copyright ©2008 by Abdo Consulting Group, Inc. International copyrights reserved in all countries.
No part of this book may be reproduced in any form without written permission from the publisher.
Abdo & Daughters™ is a trademark and logo of ABDO Publishing Company.

Printed in the United States.

Editor: John Hamilton
Graphic Design: Sue Hamilton
Cover Design: Neil Klinepier
Cover Illustration: Getty Images
Interior Photos and Illustrations: p 1 Constitution & flag, iStockphoto; p 5 teacher with apples,
Getty Images; p 6 statute of justice, iStockphoto; p 9 prisoners are loaded into a prison transport van,
AP Images; p 11 multi-racial jury, Getty Images; p 12 lawyer talks to jury, Getty Images; p 13 statue,
iStockphoto; p 15 diversified jury, Getty Images; p 17 judge, iStockphoto; p 19 Andrew Hamilton defends
John Zenger, North Wind Picture Archives; p 21 handcuffed prisoner, iStockphoto; p 22 judge with
signed plea bargain, Getty Images; p 23 detective with I.D., iStockphoto; pp 24-25 lawyer pointing, Getty
Images; p 27 police guard door, Getty Images; p 28 scales of justice, iStockphoto; p 29 judge pounding
gavel, iStockphoto; p 32 U.S. Supreme Court building, iStockphoto.

Library of Congress Cataloging-in-Publication Data

Smith, Rich, 1954-
 Sixth Amendment : the right to a fair trial / Rich Smith.
   p. cm. -- (The Bill of Rights)
 Includes index.
 ISBN 978-1-59928-918-2
 1. Fair trial--United States--Juvenile literature. 2. United States. Constitution. 6th Amendment--Juvenile
literature. 3. Due process of law--United States--Juvenile literature. 4. Speedy trial--United States--
Juvenile literature. 5. Jury--United States--Juvenile literature. 6. Right to counsel--United States--Juvenile
literature. I. Title.
 KF4765.Z9S655 2008
 347.73'5--dc22
                          2007014576

CONTENTS

INTRODUCTION

Pretend your school has started a new rule: students must bring an apple to their teachers at the beginning of class. Each class. Every day.

That could mean bringing a lot of apples with you if your school is like most others and you have five, six, or seven class periods a day. At that rate, you would need to buy as many as 35 apples a week in order to obey the new rule. Have you checked the price of apples lately? Thirty-five apples a week could cost you $20 or more. During a full year of school the cost would be somewhere between $700 and $1,000.

This causes you to ask yourself a question: "Why am I buying apples for my teachers when I could be spending that money on DVDs, or a new cell phone, or concert tickets, or great-looking shoes, and other stuff I need?" The answer you come up with makes you mad. You know the rule was started so that the teachers would feel more loved and appreciated by you and your classmates. But you can't help thinking that the teachers don't need apples for that. Telling them "thank you" ought to be more than enough. So you decide you're not going to bring apples as required.

But rules are rules. They are meant to be obeyed. Your teachers notice when you don't obey the rules, and this time is no different. Your refusal to bring apples gets you in trouble. Big trouble. You are sent to the vice principal's office. He tells you that the penalty for not bringing apples is after-school detention every day for three months, and your grade-point average reduced by half.

However, there is a way for you to avoid these penalties. You must prove that you had a good reason for not bringing the apples.

Above: What if your school had a rule that required you to bring an apple to each of your teachers every day? What if you thought the rule was unfair, and you deliberately disobeyed? Who do you think would be best to decide your innocence or guilt? Your teachers? Or your schoolmates, who have views and values similar to your own?

Above: A statue outside the U.S. Supreme Court in Washington, D.C. The Supreme Court enforces the Constitution's guarantee that all Americans accused of serious crimes have the right to have their innocence or guilt decided by people like themselves.

Let's stop the story here for a moment. Which of these two choices would be better for you? Choice One: You can explain to the vice principal your reason for not bringing apples and let him decide if it is a good enough reason to let you off the hook. Choice Two: You can explain your reason to 12 of your friends from school and let them decide as a group if it is good enough.

Having trouble choosing? Here's a hint. Most of your 12 friends don't like bringing apples either. Here's another hint. It was the vice principal who came up with the idea of bringing apples in the first place. That being the case, do you think it will be the vice principal or your friends who will be more likely to side with you and spare you from punishment? Answer: Your friends, because they share your feelings about this situation, and the vice principal doesn't.

The Founding Fathers of the United States Constitution would also very likely have picked Choice Two. We can be pretty sure about that because included in the Constitution's Bill of Rights is an amendment guaranteeing Americans accused of serious crimes the right to have their innocence or guilt decided by people like themselves, people with views and values similar to their own.

A jury is a group of people who decide innocence and guilt. They make those decisions based on evidence presented to them in a courtroom.

The Bill of Rights amendment that talks about juries and trials is the Sixth Amendment. Here is what it says: "In all criminal prosecutions, the accused shall enjoy the right to a speedy and public trial, by an impartial jury of the State and district wherein the crime shall have been committed, which district shall have been previously ascertained by law, and to be informed of the nature and cause of the accusation; to be confronted with the witnesses against him; to have compulsory process for obtaining witnesses in his favor, and to have the Assistance of Counsel for his defense."

A Joining of Minds

The Sixth Amendment right to a trial by an impartial jury is not an absolute right. That means there are situations where the government can limit that right. But the government must first have a really, really good reason for doing so.

One such limit on the Sixth Amendment is that people accused of a crime are guaranteed a jury trial only if the crime is serious. A crime is considered serious if the punishment for it requires going to prison for more than six months. Crimes for which the punishment is less than six months are called petty offenses.

There are two main reasons why there are no juries for petty offenses. The first is that it costs a great deal of money each time a jury is assembled. The government would go broke if it had to provide a jury for even the smallest of crimes. The second reason is that it takes a great deal of time to call up a jury. Having to seat a jury for each and every minor crime would clog up the court system and make speedy trials impossible.

Another limit on the Sixth Amendment has to do with where juries come from. In the early days of the United States, juries were assembled by using people who lived where the crime took place. That changed in 1904 when the Supreme Court ruled in the case of *Beavers v. Henkel* that a jury could instead come from where the criminal was charged. Say that a man who robbed a bank in San Francisco, California, was later captured in Peoria, Illinois. Before the *Beavers* case, that man would have faced trial in San Francisco, with a jury made up of people from that city. But after the *Beavers* decision, this same robber could have been tried in Peoria if that was where the charges against him were filed. But being tried before a jury of Peorians might or might not be a good thing for the accused bank robber. The reason is that the people serving on the jury in Peoria may have attitudes about crime and punishment that are different from the attitudes belonging to the jury in San Francisco.

The Sixth Amendment also requires juries to be impartial. That used to mean the jury could not be made up of people who would benefit in some way from how the trial turned out.

For example, a jury would not be impartial if one of the jurors wanted to start dating the defendant's girlfriend but could only do that if first the defendant were put behind bars for a long time.

Today, impartial still means juries must have no personal stake in the verdict. But it now also means that juries cannot reach verdicts based on the popularity or unpopularity of either the prosecutor or the defendant. In other words, jurors are not supposed to make up their minds by the way the prosecutor or defendant look, speak, or behave.

It once was thought that juries made up of fewer than 12 people were too small to be impartial. Twelve was believed to be just the right number for a proper balance of different viewpoints. Having such a balance of viewpoints would enable the jury to conduct truly reasoned discussions about the evidence, and then reach a verdict everyone could trust. That's why juries in the United States at first always had 12 members. Later, the U.S. Supreme Court decided that a jury with less than 12 could be just as fair and effective. The High Court then set the smallest legal size for a jury at six people.

Above: A prison van transports people accused of a crime. Accused prisoners may have juries made up of people from the area where their crimes took place, or from the area where the prisoners were caught.

How To Make a Fair Jury

Something the Supreme Court and others have long puzzled over is the question of how best to put together an impartial jury. Most believe the answer is to have the jury made up of people from many different walks of life. This diversity, they say, will produce a jury with the widest possible range of viewpoints and values. The thinking is that having such range will prevent the jury from being slanted in any one particular direction.

Unfortunately, it seldom works out that way in real life. In real life, people selected to be on a jury are often chosen precisely so that the jury *can be* slanted in one particular direction. What prosecutors and defense attorneys know is that some people can be counted on to think the police are heroes and can do no wrong, while others will always believe the police are villains who can do no right. A prosecutor's dream jury would be one where every juror loves the police. Their pro-police attitudes could easily cause them to assume the defendant is lying when he says he is innocent. Meanwhile, a defense attorney's dream jury would be one where every juror distrusts the police. Their anti-police attitudes could easily cause them to assume the cops are lying when claiming the defendant is guilty.

The Supreme Court says it is OK for prosecutors to attempt to shape the makeup of juries in ways that will help the government win its case against an accused person. However, the High Court also says it is OK for defense attorneys to do the same in order to help the accused person be the one who wins. The shaping of a jury is something that takes place during a process known as *voir dire*. Voir dire is French from the Latin phrase *verum dicere*, which means "an oath to speak the truth."

Above: An impartial jury is usually one made up of people from many different walks of life. This diversity helps create a jury with the widest possible range of viewpoints and values. It is hoped that this varied thinking will prevent a jury from being slanted in one direction.

Above: A lawyer speaks to a jury.

In voir dire, people who are candidates to be picked for a jury are asked questions about themselves by the prosecutor and by the defense attorney. Sometimes even the judge asks a few questions as well. These questions are meant to uncover each candidate's beliefs, opinions, and life experiences. Knowing these things can help the prosecutor and defense attorney identify candidates who will best help their case. The rules of voir dire allow both the prosecutor and defense attorney to have the least helpful candidates kept off the jury. Keeping someone off a jury is called making a *peremptory challenge*.

Prosecutors and defense attorneys can make a peremptory challenge against any juror candidate. However, it is unconstitutional to do so because of a prospective juror's race, sex, or other group-identity characteristic. As an example, assume an Hispanic defendant has been convicted of a crime by a jury that has no Hispanic members. That guilty verdict can be thrown out if the prosecutor made peremptory challenges against all Hispanic juror candidates for no reason other than their ethnicity. It is known as making a *Batson challenge* when a defendant appeals a guilty verdict on these grounds. The term Batson challenge comes from a 1986 Supreme Court ruling in the case of *Batson v. Kentucky*.

Below: A statue of blind justice. It is meant to show that in the eyes of the law, everybody is equal.

Some critics of the way juries are selected say that peremptory challenges are unfair no matter how they are used. They argue that juries would be more balanced and truly representative of the community if all of the members were simply picked at random. But those who like the idea of peremptory challenges say that verdicts are more trusted by prosecutors and defendants alike since they each had a hand in shaping the jury.

Juries Must Look Like America

PEOPLE WHO ARE CANDIDATES to be on a jury are called prospective jurors. Both the prosecutor and the defense attorney can eliminate a certain number of prospective jurors from the pool of candidates in order to produce a good jury.

However, a good jury does not have to be one made up only of people who are perfectly fair-minded. The prosecutor thinks a good jury is one made up of people who support law enforcement. The defense attorney, on the other hand, thinks a good jury is one made up of people who feel sorry for others in danger of going to prison.

The trick for the prosecutor is to eliminate from the jury anyone who might have too much sympathy for the defendant. The prosecutor can't know for certain who will or won't feel that way. But he can make very good guesses by correctly sizing up each prospective juror.

This is done by asking each candidate about his or her opinions and life experiences. Prosecutors also study prospective jurors, taking notice of how they are dressed and whether they sit up straight or slouch in their chair. These and other visual clues help the prosecutor get inside the mind of the prospective juror.

However, not all visual clues can be used by the prosecutor. The prospective juror's race is one of them. Ever since 1986, when the U.S. Supreme Court ruled in the case of *Batson v. Kentucky,* it has been a violation of the Sixth Amendment to eliminate a prospective juror from the pool of candidates because of that person's race. A convicted defendant who can prove that prospective jurors were overlooked because of their race is entitled to have his verdict of guilt thrown out.

The *Batson* case reached the Supreme Court several years after an African American man by the name of James Kirkland Batson was tried for burglary in Louisville, Kentucky. He was found guilty by a jury on which there was not a single other African American.

At the start of the trial, Batson's attorney complained to the judge about the white-only jury. He pointed out that there were four blacks among the prospective jurors and that the prosecutor deliberately excluded them. Batson's attorney argued that a jury of nothing but whites would be unable to show fairness toward an accused black man for the reason that whites have racist tendencies. The trial judge disagreed and rejected what the attorney was claiming.

After the guilty verdict, Batson's attorney appealed all the way to the U.S. Supreme Court, where at last he found sympathy for his complaint about the racial makeup of the jury. The High Court ruled that Batson's Sixth Amendment right to an impartial jury had been violated. The Supreme Court then threw out Batson's conviction and ordered a new trial.

Above: It is a violation of the Sixth Amendment to eliminate a prospective juror from a pool of candidates solely because of that person's race.

The Power of Juries To Right a Wrong

At the beginning of this book you were asked to imagine yourself refusing to obey a new school rule that forced you to bring apples to your teachers every day. You might remember that having a jury of 12 of your friends decide on your innocence or guilt was better than letting the vice principal decide. Yes, your friends might have been in agreement that you broke the school's rule by not bringing apples. But despite that, they might have voted to let you go free because they thought the rule was wrong.

This sort of thing occasionally happens in real life, in real courtroom trials. A jury that believes an accused criminal is guilty of lawbreaking but decides to proclaim him innocent because it thinks the law is unjust is said to have *nullified* that law. The power of juries to nullify law comes from the very old unwritten rule that says no jury can be jailed for the decisions it makes, not even for decisions the government dislikes or disapproves.

Of course, not everyone agrees that juries should have such power. Some argue that jurors violate their oath to uphold the law when they nullify the law. Critics wonder how fair a trial can really be if jurors are at liberty to do what they please. They also worry that the power to nullify a law in order to make a guilty defendant innocent could also be used to invent law and make an innocent defendant guilty.

Courts have attempted for many years to limit the ability of juries to use the power of nullification. For example, the U.S. Supreme Court said in the 1840 case of *Games v. Stiles ex dem Dunn* that trial judges can nullify the verdicts of juries that nullify laws and can then replace those verdicts with verdicts of their own. Then, in 1895's *Sparf v. U.S.*, the High Court said trial judges did not have to tell juries that they have the power to disregard laws they feel are unjust.

The Supreme Court has not directly ruled on the issue of nullification since then. However, a number of lower courts have. In 1997, for instance, the Second Circuit Court of Appeals held in the case of *U.S. v. Thomas* that a juror can be kicked off a jury if he or she shows signs of wanting to nullify the law. In 2001, the California Supreme Court made a similar ruling and added the requirement that jurors have a duty to warn the judge if anybody on that jury is even thinking of using nullification power.

Left: In some cases, judges can remove jurors if they show signs of wanting to nullify an existing law.

America's Most Famous Jury Rebellion

THE BEST-KNOWN CASE of an American jury rebelling against a law it thought unjust happened more than 50 years before the Sixth Amendment was written. Newspaper publisher John Peter Zenger was put on trial for a series of articles in his *New York Weekly Journal.* The articles exposed corruption on the part of New York's governor, William Cosby.

Because the articles so greatly shamed him, the governor thirsted for revenge against Zenger. He looked for a way to have the publisher thrown into prison. It would be a harsh punishment for Zenger, and it would bring an end to articles about the governor in the *Weekly Journal.*

Governor Cosby began his plot to destroy Zenger by asking a grand jury to bring charges against the German-born printer. The members of that jury said no. They didn't think Zenger or his newspaper had broken any laws in reporting on the governor's wrongdoing.

Cosby then convinced two of his most loyal judges to issue a warrant for Zenger's arrest. The charge was seditious libel. Seditious libel is a crime in which a person writes ugly lies about an official in order to make people want to rebel against him and the government.

Zenger was jailed for eight months in 1734. When his trial at last began, Zenger was defended in court by highly regarded lawyer Andrew Hamilton of Philadelphia, Pennsylvania. During the trial, Hamilton showed that the articles published by Zenger did not tell ugly lies. The very fact that the articles were true and accurate would have been enough to convince the jury of Zenger's innocence. But Hamilton went one step further. He asked the jury to also consider that the law itself was unjust. He said that an unjust law is an illegal law and one that should not be obeyed. The jury agreed with Hamilton and declared Zenger not guilty.

Above: In 1734, lawyer Andrew Hamilton defended newspaper publisher John Peter Zenger against seditious libel charges filed by New York's governor, William Cosby.

Moving Right Along

Juries can't decide someone's innocence or guilt if they don't know what crimes the defendant is accused of committing. Likewise, people on trial can't very well defend themselves if they have no idea why they are on trial.

In the centuries before the Bill of Rights, governments often arrested people and put them on trial without informing them of the charges. Governments in those days also were in the habit of arresting people and letting them rot in jail for years and years until finally getting around to having a trial. The Sixth Amendment forbids such abuses.

First, the Sixth Amendment requires that the government make sure defendants are told before a trial begins which laws they are accused of breaking. Second, the Sixth Amendment requires government to hold the trial as soon as possible after accused people are arrested. Failure to inform defendants of the charges against them, or failure to speedily start a trial, are grounds to have verdicts of guilt later thrown out if appealed to a higher court.

But just what does "speedy" mean when the Sixth Amendment says a defendant must be given a speedy trial? Does it mean the trial must begin the same day as the arrest? A week after the arrest? A month after? A year? The amendment is silent about a specific length of time, and the U.S. Supreme Court has never insisted there be one. Lawmakers in various places around the country have attempted to correct this by requiring trials to start after so many days. In the state of New York, for example, trials involving serious crimes except murder must begin within six months.

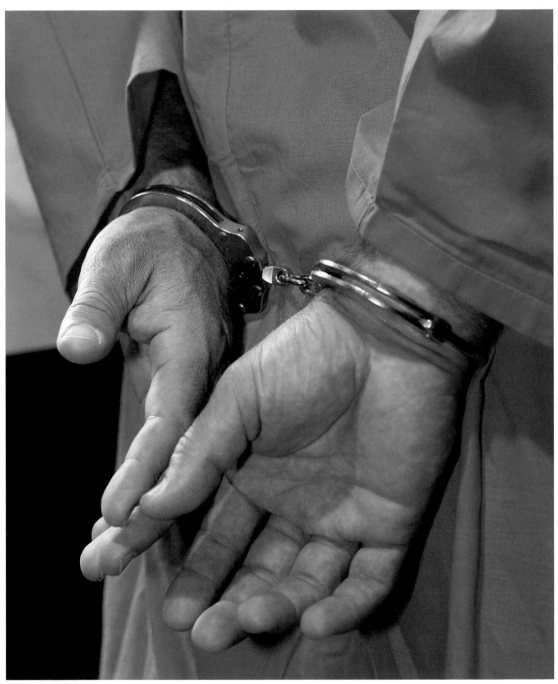

Above: Americans are guaranteed a speedy trial. However, the Sixth Amendment does not specify an exact length of time before a trial must begin.

Above: A judge holds up a signed plea bargain.

Even when start dates are set by law, there usually are situations where it is not possible to quickly go to trial. One such situation would be where there is difficulty locating important witnesses. Another would be where defense attorneys make a lengthy series of requests to establish rules for how the trial will be conducted.

Another situation that sometimes delays a trial is when the prosecutor and defendant try to reach a deal for a *plea bargain*. A plea bargain is where the defendant promises to plead guilty to crimes that carry a light punishment in exchange for the prosecutor's promise to drop charges for crimes that carry a more severe punishment. Plea bargains are often seen as smart moves for both sides in a trial. These arrangements give defendants, who believe they would be found guilty of serious charges, a way to avoid long prison sentences and quickly be done with their legal troubles. For prosecutors, plea bargains provide a sure way to win a conviction and at the same time avoid the mess and expense of a courtroom trial.

Above: A detective holds out his badge to identify himself as he searches for a witness. The search for witnesses can sometimes cause a trial to be delayed.

A Tale of Two Systems

TRIALS IN THE United States use what is known as the adversarial system of justice. It is believed that this system was developed in England sometime during the Middle Ages. In an adversarial system, an attorney who represents the government explains to a judge or jury why the person on trial should be found guilty of lawbreaking. This attorney is called a prosecutor. Sometimes the prosecutor is known as the attorney for the state, or the attorney for the people.

After the prosecutor finishes laying out the case against the person on trial, the accused then is given a chance to explain why he or she is innocent of the charges. This person is called a defendant. The defendant's case is usually presented by an attorney hired to speak and argue on his or her behalf. This attorney is sometimes referred to as the defendant's advocate, or counsel.

Outside the United States, many countries hold trials that use what is known as an inquisitorial system of justice. This system, as used on the continent of Europe, began in the Roman Empire and was updated during the time of Napoleon. In an inquisitorial system, the job of the prosecutor is performed by one or more judges. Juries are almost never used. The inquisitorial system is less concerned about providing a fair trial than it is about gathering enough facts in a case so that the judges can reach a verdict.

Many people believe the adversarial system is the better of the two ways to conduct trials because it is fairer than the inquisitorial system. However, some critics find plenty to dislike about the adversarial system. Their main complaint is that the

Above: A lawyer pleads his client's case.

side most likely to win a trial is the one with the smartest attorney, a lawyer with the most courtroom experience and the greatest ability to sway juries. Unfortunately, such attorneys are very expensive. Critics of the system say this puts defendants who are poor at a big disadvantage. They say that defendants without money cannot afford a lawyer with the kind of skills needed to keep them from being found guilty.

NOTHING HIDDEN

The Sixth Amendment also requires that trials be open to the public. The authors of the Bill of Rights wanted public trials because they knew it would help keep things honest. They remembered the times before the United States became a country when trials were often held in secret. It's easy for courts to skip certain important steps during a trial when no one from the public is allowed to watch. For example, defendants can be boldly cheated of their right to call witnesses who might help prove their innocence.

However, there are a very few times when it's OK for a trial to be closed to the public. A trial can be closed if the evidence presented will expose secret national-security information. In such a circumstance, the government's duty to keep the nation safe will be seen as being more important than any single person's right to an open trial. A trial also can be closed if having the public attend will in some way hurt a defendant's right to a fair trial.

Another important guarantee of the Sixth Amendment is the accused person's right to be defended by an attorney of his or her choosing. The Supreme Court long ago ruled that the Sixth Amendment's guarantee of an attorney requires the government to pay for one if a defendant doesn't have the money to hire a lawyer.

Lastly, the Sixth Amendment promises that government cannot stop defendants from confronting witnesses who testify against them. In a trial, the confronting of witnesses is called cross-examination. What defendants and their attorneys attempt to do during cross-examination is poke holes in the testimony of prosecution witnesses. The goal is to show that these witnesses have given testimony that is

wrong or simply not believable. This is done by asking the right kinds of questions. For example, a prosecution witness might testify that he saw the defendant holding a gun in his hand at the time of the murder. Under skillful cross-examination, the witness could be asked questions that force him to admit that the "gun" he saw may have been nothing more than a wallet.

Above: A trial can be closed if the evidence presented will expose secret national-security information.

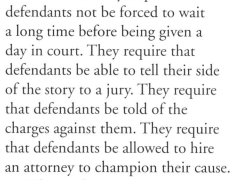

SAFEGUARDING LIBERTY

Below: In the United States, every effort is made to keep the scales of justice balanced so that an accused person receives a fair trial.

It's no fun to be accused of a crime. Especially a crime you know you did not commit. In many places around the world, to be accused of a crime is the same thing as being found guilty of it. That's why you are very fortunate if you live in the United States. Few other countries are as careful as the United States when it comes to the way their criminal and civil trials are conducted. America values fairness. For that reason, its courts follow strict rules when putting an accused person on trial.

Among the most important of those rules are the ones listed in the Sixth Amendment. They require that defendants not be forced to wait a long time before being given a day in court. They require that defendants be able to tell their side of the story to a jury. They require that defendants be told of the charges against them. They require that defendants be allowed to hire an attorney to champion their cause.

These rules exist not just to make sure court trials are fair. They also exist to safeguard your liberty. The liberty you have is something you were born with. The job of the Sixth Amendment is to make sure government remembers your liberties any time you are led into a courtroom.

Above: Americans value fairness in their court trials. Under the Sixth Amendment, all defendants accused of a serious crime are guaranteed a speedy trial where they can tell their side of the story to a judge and jury.

GLOSSARY

Amendment

When it was created, the Constitution wasn't perfect. The Founding Fathers wisely added a special section. It allowed the Constitution to be changed by future generations. This makes the Constitution flexible. It is able to bend to the will of the people it governs. Changes to the Constitution are called amendments. The first 10 amendments are called the Bill of Rights. An amendment must be approved by two-thirds of both houses of Congress. Once that happens, the amendment must be approved by three-fourths of the states. Then it becomes law. This is a very difficult thing to do. The framers of the Constitution didn't want it changed unless there was a good reason. There have been over 9,000 amendments proposed. Only 27 of them have been ratified, or made into law. Some amendments changed the way our government works. The Twelfth Amendment changed the way we elect our president. The Twenty-Second Amendment limits a president to two terms in office. Constitutional amendments have also increased the freedoms of our citizens. The Thirteenth Amendment finally got rid of slavery. And the Nineteenth Amendment gave women the right to vote.

Bill of Rights

The first 10 amendments to the United States Constitution make up what is known as the Bill of Rights. The Bill of Rights lists the special freedoms every human is born with and is able to enjoy in America. Also, the Bill of Rights tells the government that it cannot stop people from fully using and enjoying those freedoms unless the government has an extremely good reason for doing so.

Defendant

A person, business, or government entity (such as a corporation or town) accused of doing something wrong. In a jury trial, defendants try to defend themselves against the charge or charges placed against them.

Founding Fathers

The men who participated in the Constitutional Convention in 1787, especially the ones who signed the Constitution. Some of the Founding Fathers included George Washington, Benjamin Franklin, John Rutledge, Gouverneur Morris, Alexander Hamilton, and James Madison.

High Court

Another name for the United States Supreme Court.

Jury

A group of ordinary people from all walks of life who make decisions based on evidence presented to them. There are two types of juries. A *petit* jury usually consists of between 9 and 12 people who meet in a courtroom to decide on the guilt or innocence of individuals accused of a crime. Petit juries are usually the kind seen in courtroom dramas on TV or in the movies. Another type of jury is the *grand* jury. This is a group of 12 to 23 people. A grand jury decides whether there is enough evidence against a suspected lawbreaker to have a court trial. The importance of grand juries is that they help make sure prosecutors act honestly and fairly when building a case against someone they accuse of the most serious types of crimes. This helps protect against out-of-control prosecutors trying to send innocent people to prison.

Prosecution

A person or group who brings charges of wrong-doing against another person, business, or government entity (defendant). These charges may lead to a trial taking place. During this trial, the prosecution will try to prove that the defendant is guilty.

Supreme Court

The United States Supreme Court is the highest court in the country. There are nine judges on the Supreme Court. They make sure local, state, and federal governments are following the rules spelled out in the United States Constitution. Our understanding of the Constitution evolves over time. It is up to the Supreme Court to decide how the Constitution is applied to today's society. When the Supreme Court rules on a case, other courts in the country must follow the decision in similar situations. In this way, the laws of the Constitution are applied equally to all Americans.

Verdict

A jury's decision as to whether a defendant is guilty or innocent in a court trial. The jury comes to this decision after reviewing all the facts of a case made by the defendant and the prosecution.

Witness

A person who swears under oath to tell the truth about something they've seen, heard, or experienced.

INDEX

The U.S. Supreme Court building in Washington, D.C.